HOSTING *the* PRESENCE

LEADER'S GUIDE

Destiny Image Books by Bill Johnson

A Life of Miracles

Dreaming With God

Center of the Universe

Momentum

Release the Power of Jesus

Strengthen Yourself in the Lord

The Supernatural Power of a Transformed Mind

Hosting the Presence

LEADER'S GUIDE

Bill Johnson

HOSTING *the* PRESENCE

Unveiling Heaven's Agenda

DESTINY IMAGE® PUBLISHERS, INC.
P.O. Box 310, Shippensburg, PA 17257-0310
"Promoting Inspired Lives."

This book and all other Destiny Image, Revival Press, MercyPlace, Fresh Bread, Destiny Image Fiction, and Treasure House books are available at Christian bookstores and distributors worldwide.

For a U.S. bookstore nearest you, call 1-800-722-6774.
For more information on foreign distributors, call 717-532-3040.
Reach us on the Internet: www.destinyimage.com.

ISBN 13 TP: 978-0-7684-4235-9

For Worldwide Distribution, Printed in the U.S.A.
1 2 3 4 5 6 7 8 / 17 16 15 14 13

CONTENTS

BASIC LEADER GUIDELINES

This study is designed to take you from being a Christian who has the Holy Spirit living inside of you to a history maker who recognizes and releases this incredible gift of Christ-in-you. The Holy Spirit is in you...*and He wants out!*

There are several different ways that you can engage this study. By no means is this forthcoming list comprehensive. Rather, these are the standard outlets recommended to facilitate this curriculum. We encourage you to seek the Lord's direction, be creative, and prepare for supernatural transformation in your Christian life.

When all is said and done, this curriculum is unique in that the end goal is *not* information—it is hunger. The sessions are intentionally sequenced to take every believer on a journey from information to revelation to hunger, which will lead to a greater encounter with God's Presence than they have ever experienced before.

Here are some of the ways you can use the curriculum:

I. CHURCH SMALL GROUP

Often, churches feature a variety of different small group opportunities per season, in terms of books, curriculum resources, and Bible studies. *Hosting the Presence* would be included among the offering of titles for whatever season you are launching the small group program.

It is recommended that you have at least four to five people to make up a small group, and a maximum of twelve. If you end up with more than twelve members, either the group needs to multiply and break into two different groups, or you should consider moving toward a church class model (which will be outlined next).

For a small group setting, here are the essentials:

- Meeting place: Either the leader's home, or a space provided by the church.

- Appropriate technology: A DVD player attached to a TV that is large enough for all of the group members to see (and loud enough for everyone to hear).
- Leader/Facilitator: This person will often be the host, if the small group is being conducted at someone's home; but it can also be a team (husband/wife, two church leaders, etc.). The leader(s) will direct the session from beginning to end, from sending reminder e-mails to participating group members about the meetings, to closing out the sessions in prayer and dismissing everyone. That said, leaders can select certain people in the group to assist with various elements of the meeting: worship, prayer, ministry time, etc. A detailed description of what the group meetings should look like will follow in the pages to come.

Sample Schedule for Home Group Meeting (for a 7:00 P.M. Meeting)

- Before arrival: Ensure that refreshments are ready by 6:15 P.M. If they need to be refrigerated, ensure they are preserved appropriately until 15 minutes prior to the official meeting time.
- 6:15 P.M.: Leaders arrive at meeting home or facility.
- 6:15–6:25 P.M.: Connect with hosts, co-hosts, and/or co-leaders to review the evening's program.
- 6:25–6:35 P.M.: Pray with hosts, co-hosts, and/or co-leaders for the evening's events. Here are some sample prayer directives:
    - For the Holy Spirit to move and minister freely.
    - For the teaching to connect with and transform all who hear it.
    - For dialogue and conversation that edifies.
    - For comfort and transparency among group members.
    - For the Presence of God to manifest during worship.
    - For testimonies of answered prayers.
    - For increased hunger for God's Presence.
- 6:35–6:45: Ensure technology is functioning properly!
    - Test the DVDs featuring the teaching sessions, making sure they are set up to the appropriate session.
    - If you are doing praise and worship, ensure that either the MP3 player or CD

player is functional, set at an appropriate volume (not soft, but not incredibly loud), and that song sheets are available for everyone so they can sing along with the lyrics. (If you are tech savvy, you could do a PowerPoint or Keynote presentation featuring the lyrics.)

- 6:45–7:00 P.M.: Welcome and greeting for guests.
- 7:00–7:10 P.M.: Fellowship, community, and refreshments.
- 7:10–7:12 P.M.: Gather everyone together in the meeting place.
- 7:12–7:30 P.M.: Introductory prayer and worship.
- 7:30–7:40 P.M.: Ministry and prayer time.
- 7:40–8:00 P.M.: Watch DVD session.
- 8:00–8:20 P.M.: Discuss DVD session.
- 8:20–8:35 P.M.: Activation time.
- 8:35–8:40 P.M.: Closing prayer and dismiss.

This sample schedule is *not* intended to lock you into a formula. It is simply provided as a template to help you get started. Our hope is that you customize it according to the unique needs of your group, and sensitively navigate the activity of the Holy Spirit as He uses these sessions to supernaturally transform the lives of every person participating in the study.

2. Small Group Church-Wide Campaign

This would be the decision of the pastor or senior leadership of the church. In this model, the entire church would go through *Hosting the Presence* in both the main services and ancillary small groups/life classes.

These campaigns would be marketed as *40 Days of Presence* or *40 Days of Hosting the Presence.* The pastor's weekend sermon would be based on the principles in *Hosting the Presence*, and the Sunday school classes/life classes and/or small groups would also follow the *Hosting the Presence* curriculum.

3. Church Class | Midweek Class | Sunday School Curriculum

Churches of all sizes offer a variety of classes purposed to develop members into more effective disciples of Jesus and agents of transformation in their spheres of influence.

Hosting the Presence would be an invaluable addition to a church's class offering. Typically, churches offer a variety of topical classes, targeted at men's needs, women's needs, marriage, family, finances, and various areas of Bible study.

Hosting the Presence is a unique resource, as it does not fit in with the aforementioned traditional topics. On the contrary, this study breaks down a foundational truth of the Christian life—what it means to be indwelt by the Holy Spirit—and takes it to a whole new level for all believers, showing them how to steward God's Presence and supernaturally transform their worlds.

Believers are often acquainted with the "101" understanding, that because they are born again they have received the Holy Spirit. They may have even gone through a new members' class or basic discipleship course that provided an essential foundation of who the Holy Spirit is, and how the process of being born again works.

The benefit of *Hosting the Presence* is that it builds on *whatever* foundation a believer may have already received about the Holy Spirit—whether the information they received was extremely basic, or they were taken further down the road and given some instruction on the baptism of the Holy Spirit. Either way, *Hosting the Presence* ideally builds on the foundation, taking Christians from being Spirit-indwelt to becoming Presence-empowered.

While it may be difficult to facilitate dialogue in a class setting, it is certainly optional and recommended. The other way to successfully engage *Hosting the Presence* in a class setting is to have a teacher/leader go through the questions/answers presented in the upcoming pages and use these as his or her teaching notes.

4. Individual Study

While the curriculum is designed for use in a group setting, it also works as a tool that can equip anyone who is looking to go deeper in his or her experience of God's Presence.

STEPS TO LAUNCHING A *HOSTING THE PRESENCE* GROUP OR CLASS

PREPARE WITH PRAYER!

- Pray! If you are a church leader, prayerfully consider how *Hosting the Presence* could transform the culture and climate of your church community. The Lord is raising up bodies of believers that, above all, relentlessly pursue and release God's Presence in their unique spheres of influence. Spend some time with the Holy Spirit, asking Him to give you vision for what this unique study will do for your church, and, ultimately, how a Presence-focused people will transform your city and region.
- If you are a **group leader** or **class facilitator**, pray for those who will be attending your group, signing up for your class, and positioning their lives to be transformed by the power and Presence of God in this study.

PREPARE PRACTICALLY!

- Determine how you will be using the *Hosting the Presence* curriculum.
- Identify which of the following formats you will be using the curriculum in:
    - Church-sponsored small group study.
    - Church-wide campaign.
    - Church class (Wednesday night, Sunday morning, etc.).
    - Individual study.
- Determine a meeting location and ensure availability of appropriate equipment.

- Keep in mind the number of people who may attend. You will also need AV (audiovisual) equipment. The more comfortable the setting, the more people will enjoy being there, and will spend more time ministering to each other!
- Just a word of caution here: the larger the group, the greater your need for co-leaders or assistants. The ideal small group size is difficult to judge; however, once you get more than 10-12 people, it becomes difficult for each member to feel "heard." If your group is larger than 12 people, consider either having two or more small group discussion leaders, or "multiplying" the larger group into two smaller ones.

▪ Determine the format for your meetings.

- The Presence of the Lord is cradled and stewarded well in the midst of organization. Structure should never replace spontaneity, but, on the contrary, having a plan and determining what type of format your meetings will take will enable you to flow with the Holy Spirit and minister more effectively.
- Also, by determining what kind of meeting you will be hosting, you become better equipped to develop a schedule for the meeting, identify potential co-leaders, and order the appropriate quantity of resources.

▪ Set a schedule for your meetings.

- Once you have established the format for your meetings, set a schedule for your meetings. Some groups like to have a time of fellowship or socializing, either before or after the meeting begins, where light refreshments are offered. Some groups will want to incorporate times of worship and personal ministry into the small group or class. This is highly recommended for *Hosting the Presence*, as the study is designed to equip and activate believers through encountering God's Presence. The video portion and discussion questions are intended to equip believers, while the worship, times of ministry, group interaction, prayer time, and activation element are purposed to puts hands and feet to the material covered.
- Hosting God's Presence is not a lofty theological concept; it is a practical reality for every born-again believer. This study is intended to educate; but even more so, it is designed to activate believers and position them to steward the transformative Presence of God in their unique spheres of influence.

▪ Establish a start date along with a weekly meeting day and time.

- This eight-week curriculum should be followed consistently and consecutively. Be mindful of the fact that while there are eight weeks of material, most groups will want to meet one last time after completing the last week to celebrate, or designate their first meeting as a time to get to know each other and "break the ice." This is very normal and should be encouraged to continue the community momentum that the small group experience initiates. Typically, after the final session is completed, groups will often engage in a social activity—either going out to dinner together, seeing a movie, or something of the like.

- Look far enough ahead on the calendar to account for anything that might interfere. Choose a day that works well for the members of your group. For a church class, be sure to coordinate the time with the appropriate ministry leader.

- Advertise!
    - Group/Class Leaders, visit the website www.hostingthepresence.com to access special resources that will help you to effectively promote the course and communicate with group members. Getting the word out in multiple ways is most effective. Print up flyers, post a sign-up sheet, make an announcement in church services or group meetings, send out weekly e-mails and text messages, set up your own blog or website, or post the event on the social media avenue you and your group utilize most (Facebook, Twitter, etc.). A personal invitation or phone call is a great way to reach those who might need that little bit of extra encouragement.
    - For any type of small group or class to succeed, it must be endorsed by and encouraged from the leadership. For larger churches with multiple group/class offerings, it is wise to provide church members literature featuring all of the different small group/class options. This information should also be featured online in an easily accessible page on your church website.
    - For smaller churches, it is a good idea for the pastor or a key leader to announce the launch of a small group course or class from the pulpit during an announcement time.

- Gather your materials.
    - Each leader will need the *Hosting the Presence Leader's Kit*, as well as the *Hosting the Presence* book.
    - Additionally, each participant will need a personal copy of the *Hosting the Presence Workbook*. It is recommended they also purchase the *Hosting the Presence* book for further enrichment and as a resource to complement their daily readings. However, they are able to engage the exercises and participate in the group discussion apart from reading the book.

- We have found it best for the materials to all be purchased at one time—many booksellers and distributors offer discounts on multiple orders, and you are assured that each member will have their materials from the beginning.

STEP FORWARD!

- Arrive at your meeting in plenty of time to prepare; frazzled last-minute preparations do not put you in a place of "rest," and your group members will sense your stress! Ensure that all AV equipment is working properly, and that you have ample supplies for each member. Name tags are a great idea, at least for the first couple of meetings. Icebreaker and introduction activities are also a good idea for the first meeting.
- Pray for your members. As much as possible, make yourself available to them. As each person increases in revelation and understanding of the Holy Spirit's Presence upon their lives, they will want to share that discovery! You will also need to encourage those who struggle, grow weary, or lose heart. Make sure your members stay committed so they experience the full benefits of this teaching.
- Embrace the supernatural journey that you and your fellow members are embarking on to carry and release God's Presence! Transformation begins within you!
- Multiply yourself. Is there someone you know who was not able to attend your group? Help them to initiate their own small group now that you know how effective hosting God's Presence can be in a group setting!

THANK YOU

Thank you for embarking on a journey that will sow into a true modern reformation, and ultimately position you to be an agent of supernatural change wherever God has placed you.

Remember, all believers have received the Holy Spirit. There is no begging, bargaining, or pleading that needs to be done with God in order for Him to release this gift. His hands are not clenched around His Presence. It has been freely given to all who have trusted in Jesus as their Lord and Savior. That is settled.

That said, many believers live their entire Christian lives without ever experiencing the power of the Spirit *upon them*. As Pastor Bill Johnson often says, "He (the Holy Spirit) lives in me for my sake; but He is upon me for your sake." That is the journey you are going on. The Spirit of God lives in every believer; however, He also longs to rest upon every believer and release the Kingdom in every life, every church, every city, and every sphere of society, that His glory would cover the earth!

LEADER CHECKLIST

ONE TO TWO MONTHS PRIOR

- ______ Have you determined a start date for your class or small group?
- ______ Have you determined the format, meeting day and time, and weekly meeting schedule?
- ______ Have you selected a meeting location (making sure you have adequate space and AV equipment available)?
- ______ Have you advertised? Do you have a sign-up sheet to ensure you order enough materials?

TWO WEEKS TO ONE MONTH PRIOR

- ______ Have your ordered materials? You will need a copy of the *Hosting the Presence Leader's Kit,* along with copies of the workbook and book for each participant.
- ______ Have you organized your meeting schedule/format?

ONE TO TWO WEEKS PRIOR

- ______ Have you received all your materials?
- ______ Have you reviewed the DVDs and your Leader's Guide to familiarize yourself with the material, and to ensure everything is in order?
- ______ Have you planned and organized your refreshments, if you are planning to provide them? Some leaders will handle this themselves, and some find it easier to allow participants to sign up to provide refreshments if they would like to do so.

- ______ Have you advertised and promoted? This includes sending out e-mails to all participants, setting up a Facebook group, setting up a group through your church's database system (if available), promotion in the church bulletin, etc.
- ______ Have you appointed co-leaders to assist you with the various portions of the group/class? While it is not necessary, it is helpful to have someone who is in charge of either leading (on guitar, keyboard, etc.) or arranging the worship music (putting songs on a CD, creating lyric sheets, etc.). It is also helpful to have a prayer coordinator—someone who helps facilitate the prayer time, ensuring that all of the prayer needs are acknowledged and remembered and assigning the various requests to group members who would be willing to lift up those needs in prayer.

First Meeting Day

- Plan to arrive EARLY! Give yourself extra time to set up the meeting space, double-check all AV equipment, and organize your materials. It might be helpful to ask participants to arrive 15 minutes early for the first meeting to allow for distribution of materials and any icebreaker activity you might have planned.

Weekly Overview of Meetings/ Group Sessions

Here are some instructions on how to use each of the weekly Discussion Question guides.

Welcome and Fellowship Time (10-15 Minutes)

This usually begins five to ten minutes prior to the designated meeting time, and typically continues up until ten minutes after the official starting time. Community is important. One of the issues in many small group/class environments is the lack of connectivity. People walk around inspired and resourced, but they remain disconnected from other believers. Foster an environment where community is welcome but, at the same time, not distracting. This tends to be a problem that plagues small group settings more than classes.

Welcome everyone as they walk in. If it is a small group environment, as the host or leader, be intentional about connecting with each person as they enter the meeting space. If it is a church class environment, it is still recommended that the leader connect with each participant. However, there will be less pressure for the participants to feel connected immediately in a traditional class setting versus a more intimate, small group environment.

Have refreshments and materials ready. In the small group, you can serve refreshments and facilitate fellowship between group members. In a class setting, talk with the attendees and ensure that they purchase all of their necessary materials (workbook and copy of *Hosting the Presence*). Ideally, the small group members will have received their resources prior to Week 1, but if not, ensure that the materials are present at the meeting and available for group members to pick up. It is advisable that you have several copies of the workbook and book available at the small group meeting just in case people did not pick up their copies at the designated time.

Call the meeting to order. This involves gathering everyone together in the appropriate place and clearly stating that the meeting is getting ready to start.

Pray! Open every session in prayer, specifically addressing the topic that you will be covering in the upcoming meeting time. Invite the manifest Presence of the Holy Spirit to come, move among the group members, minister to them individually, reveal Jesus, and stir greater hunger in each participant to experience *more* of God's Presence in their lives.

Introductions (10 Minutes—First Class Only)

While a time of formal introduction should only be done on the first week of the class/session, it is recommended that in subsequent meetings group members state their names when addressing a question, making a prayer request, giving a comment, etc., just to ensure that everyone is familiar with each other's names. You are also welcome to do a short icebreaker activity.

- (First Meeting) Introduce yourself, and allow each participant to briefly introduce himself or herself. This should work fine for both small group and class environments. In a small group, you can go around the room and have each person introduce him- or herself one at a time. In a classroom setting, establish some type of flow and then have each person give a quick introduction (name, interesting factoid, etc.).
- (First Meeting) Discuss the schedule for the meetings. Provide participants an overview of what the next eight weeks will look like. If you plan to do any type of "social activities," you might want to advertise that right off the bat, noting that while the curriculum runs for eight weeks, there will be a ninth session dedicated to fellowship and some type of fun activity.
- (First Meeting) Distribute materials to each participant. Briefly orient the participants to the book and workbook, explaining the 15-20 minute time commitment for each day. Encourage each person to engage fully in this journey—they will get out of it only as much as they invest. The purpose for the daily reinforcement activities is not to add busywork to their lives. This is actually a way to cultivate a habit of Bible study and daily time pursuing God's Presence, starting with just 15-20 minutes a day. Morning, evening, afternoon—when does not matter. The key is making the decision to engage.

Worship (15 Minutes—Optional for the First Meeting)

Fifteen minutes is a solid time for a worship segment. That said, it all depends upon the culture of your group. If everyone is okay with doing 30 minutes of praise and worship, by all means, go for it.

For this curriculum, a worship segment is highly recommended as the focus for each session is increasing a believer's hunger for more of God's Presence. Worship is a fundamental gateway to experiencing the very person the *Hosting the Presence* curriculum pursues.

If a group chooses to do a worship segment, often they decide to begin on the second week. It usually takes an introductory meeting for everyone to become acquainted with one another and comfortable with their surroundings before they open up in worship.

On the other hand, if the group members are already comfortable with one another and they are ready to launch right into a time of worship, they should definitely begin on the first meeting.

While it has been unusual for Sunday school/church classes to engage worship in their sessions, it is actually a powerful way to prepare participants to receive the truth being shared in the *Hosting the Presence* sessions. In addition, pre-service worship (if the class is being held prior to a Sunday morning worship experience), actually stirs hunger in the participants for greater encounters, both corporately and congregationally, in God's Presence.

If the class is held midweek (or on a day where there is *no* church service going on), a praise and worship component is a wonderful way to refresh believers in God's Presence as they are given the privilege of coming together midweek, and corporately experiencing His Presence in worship.

Prayer/Ministry Time (5-15 Minutes)

At this point, you will transition from either welcome or worship into a time of prayer.

Just like praise and worship, it is recommended that this initial time of prayer be five to ten minutes in length; but if the group is made up of people who do not mind praying longer, than it should not be discouraged. The key is stewarding everyone's time well while maintaining focus on the most important things.

Prayer should be navigated carefully, as there will always be people who use it as an opportunity to speak longer than they ought, complain about circumstances in their lives, or potentially even gossip about other people.

At the same time, there are real people sharing deep, legitimate needs sharing deep, legitimate needs with the group that need supernatural ministry. the group that need supernatural ministry. This time is for them to not only receive prayer, but to also learn how to exercise Jesus' authority in their own lives and see their impossible situations bow in His Presence, at His Name.

This prayer time doubles as a "ministry time," when believers are encouraged to flow in the gifts of the Holy Spirit. After the door is opened through worship, the atmosphere is typically charged with God's Presence. It is quite common for people to receive words of knowledge, words of wisdom, prophetic words, and for other manifestations of the Holy Spirit to take place (see 1 Cor. 12). This is a safe environment for people to "practice" these gifts, take risks, etc. However, if there are people who demonstrate consistent disorder, are unceasingly distracting, have problems/issues that move beyond the scope of this particular curriculum (and appear to need specialized counseling), or have issues that veer more into the theological realm, it is best for you to refer these people to an appropriate leader in the church.

If you are such a leader, you can either point them to a different person, or you can encourage them to save their questions/comments and you will address them outside of the group, as you do not want to distract from what God is doing in these moments, specifically, for these people.

Transition Time

At this point, you will transition from prayer/ministry time to watching the *Hosting the Presence* DVDs.

Group leaders/class teachers: It is recommended that you have the DVD in the player and all ready to press "PLAY" on the appropriate session at the beginning of the meeting.

Video/Teaching (20-25 Minutes)

During this time, group members will fill in the blanks in their participant workbooks. All of the information they need to complete this assignment will appear on-screen, during the session. However, there will be additional information that appears on-screen that will *not* go in the "fill in the blank" section. This is simply for the viewers' own notation.

Discussion Questions (20-30 Minutes)

In the *Leader's Guide*, each question will look like the following (see example below from Week 1):

- *Read Genesis 1:27-28.* Why did God instruct Adam and Eve to fill and *subdue* the earth?

    - ANSWER: He instructed them to subdue the earth (*subdue* being a military term) because they were God's ambassadors—purposed and equipped to exercise His authority over the serpent in the Garden. As they populated the world beyond the confines of the Garden, they were bound to deal with the chaos created by satan and his rebellion. God was commissioning them to reclaim areas beyond the Garden that had become infected by darkness.

Some lessons will have more questions than others. The first few lessons have less subjective questions ("you and me" types of questions where people recount their personal experiences) than the following lessons. Also, there might be some instances where you choose to cut certain questions out for the sake of time. This is entirely up to you, and in a circumstance where the Holy Spirit is moving and appears to be focusing on some questions more than others, flow in sync with the Holy Spirit. He will not steer you wrong!

First, you will have a question. Typically, it will lead with a Scripture verse (but not always). To engage group members, you can ask for volunteers to read the Scripture verse(s). As you ask the question in the group setting, encourage more than one person to provide an answer. Usually, you will have some people who are way off in their responses, but you will also have those who provide *part* of the correct answer.

Second, we have provided a sample answer—which is one of the most concise responses in how to appropriately answer the question. This is a tool to help you navigate the conversation and ensure that everyone is on the same page when it comes to understanding the topic that the particular session covered. *Be sure to study and review the answer* so you are ready to respond to questions and field the answers provided by the group members.

Third, there is a very intentional flow in the order of questions. The questions will usually start out by addressing a problem, misconception, or false understanding, and are designed to take believers to a point of informationally addressing the problem, and then, taking action.

The problem with many curriculum studies is in the question/answer section. Participants may feel like the conversation was lively, the dialogue insightful, and that the meeting was an overall success; but when all is said and done, the question, *"What do I do next?"* is not sufficiently answered.

This is why every discussion time will be followed with an activation segment.

Activate (5-10 Minutes)

- Each activation segment should be five to ten minutes at the minimum, as this is the place where believers start putting to action what they just learned.
- The activation segment will be custom-tailored for the session covered.
- Even though every group member might not be able to participate in the activation exercise, it gives them a visual for what the expression of the concept they just learned about should look like.

TAKE AWAY

After the activation exercise, we have included a brief summary of the "Take Away" from that unique session. This is what the participants should walk away from the sessions—knowing and applying.

Plans for the Next Week (2 Minutes)

Remind group members about daily exercises in the workbook. Encourage everyone to participate fully in this journey in order to get the most out of it. The daily exercises should not take more than 15-20 minutes and they will make a fantastic 40-day themed Bible study.

Be sure to let group members know if the meeting location will change or differ from week to week, or if there are any other pertinent announcements to your group/class. Weekly e-mails, Facebook updates, and text messages are great tools to communicate with your group. If your church has a database tool that allows for communication between small group/class leaders and members, that works exceptionally well.

Close in Prayer

Good opportunity to ask for a volunteer.

Week 1

YOUR AUTHORITY TO RELEASE GOD'S PRESENCE

Prayer Focus: Ask the Lord to give every participant a strong foundation in the subject of the believer's authority.

Fellowship, Welcome, and Introductions (20-30 Minutes—For the First Meeting)

- Welcome everyone as they walk in. If it is a small group environment, as the host or leader, be intentional about connecting with each person as they come to the meeting space. If it is a church class environment, it is still recommended that the leader connect with each participant. However, there will be less pressure for the participants to feel connected immediately in a traditional class setting versus a more intimate, small group environment.
- In the small group, serve refreshments and facilitate fellowship between group members. In a class setting, talk with the attendees and ensure that they receive all of their necessary materials (the workbook and a copy of *Hosting the Presence*).
- Introduce yourself, and allow each participant to briefly introduce themselves. This should work fine for both small group and class environments. In a small group, you can go around the room and have each person introduce him- or herself one at a time. In a classroom setting, establish some type of flow and then have each person give a quick introduction (name, interesting factoid, etc.).
- Discuss the schedule for the meetings. Provide participants an overview of what the next eight weeks will look like. If you plan to do any type of "social activities," you might want to advertise that right off the bat, noting that while the curriculum runs for eight weeks, there will be a ninth session dedicated to fellowship and some type of fun activity. However, you may come up with this idea later on in the actual study.

- Distribute materials to each participant. Briefly orient the participants to the book and workbook, explaining the 15-20 minute time commitment for each day. Encourage each person to engage fully in this journey—they will get out of it only as much as they invest. The purpose for the daily reinforcement activities is not to add busywork to their lives. This is actually a way to cultivate a habit of Bible study and daily time pursuing God's Presence, starting with just 15-20 minutes. Morning, evening, afternoon—when does not matter. The key is making the decision to engage.

Opening Prayer

Worship (15 Minutes—Optional for First Meeting)

If a group chooses to do a worship segment, often they decide to begin on the second week. It usually takes an introductory meeting for everyone to become acquainted with one another and comfortable with their surroundings before they open up in worship.

On the other hand, if the group members are already comfortable with one another and they are ready to launch right into a time of worship, they should definitely go for it!

Prayer/Ministry Time (5-15 Minutes)

Video/Teaching (20 Minutes)

Discussion Questions (25-30 Minutes)

- *Read Genesis 1:27-28.* Why did God instruct Adam and Eve to fill and *subdue* the earth?

    - ANSWER: He instructed them to subdue the earth (*subdue* being a military term) because they were God's ambassadors—purposed and equipped to exercise His authority over the serpent in the Garden. As they populated the world beyond the confines of the Garden, they were certain to deal with the chaos created by satan and his rebellion. God was commissioning them to reclaim areas beyond the Garden that had become infected by darkness.

- *Read Romans 6:16.* How did mankind become a "slave to sin"? What did sin establish between man and the devil?

    - ANSWER: Mankind became a slave to sin when he disobeyed God in the Garden.

    - Sin made mankind subject to the devil—the author of sin—and, therefore, the enemy became mankind's ruthless taskmaster.

- *Read Luke 4:5-6.* How was the devil able to offer Jesus "the kingdoms of the world" during the wilderness temptation?
  - ANSWER: The devil became the "god of this world" when mankind gave him legal access to the kingdoms of the world in Eden through agreement.
- *Read Matthew 28:18-19.* In the Great Commission, Jesus said that "all authority" was given to Him. What does this mean for the enemy?
  - ANSWER: If Jesus has all authority, the enemy has none!
- Jesus said that He has all authority, and has commissioned the Church to "Go" and disciple nations with that authority. If we have access to Jesus' authority, what does that mean when it comes to us dealing with the enemy?
  - ANSWER: Jesus has all authority. Jesus lives in us and through us by the Holy Spirit. Therefore, we have legal access to Jesus' authority and are able to exercise it over every power of the enemy.
- *Read John 5:19 and John 14:12.* How did Jesus perform His miracles? And what are the implications for you today?
  - ANSWER: As a man anointed by the Holy Spirit.
  - Since Jesus did miracles because the Spirit anointed Him, we are able to model Him and work the same kinds of miracles...and even *greater works*...since we have received the same Holy Spirit.

Activate: Exercise Your Authority! (10 Minutes)

- Ask group/class members if there are areas in their lives that they need to exercise authority over (sickness, torment, fear, trauma, etc.).
- Remind the group/class that nothing Jesus did is off limits to them; remember, He ministered supernaturally because the Holy Spirit anointed Him. If they are born again, they are anointed by the same Spirit to do the same works that Jesus did! If they are not yet saved, now is as good a time as any to introduce them to King Jesus!
- Have the group/class members pray for each other, recognizing that Jesus has all authority and the enemy has no authority!

TAKE AWAY

To become world changers, it is important that we first recognize the authority we have received and exercise it in our own lives to experience breakthrough. It cannot be a concept or teaching; it must be the reality we walk in as normal Christianity! We have been freely given God's Presence so that we can freely release it to others.

Plans for the Next Week (2 Minutes)

Point out Day 1 through Day 5 in the workbook. Encourage everyone to participate fully in this daily journey in order to get the most out of it.

Close in Prayer

Week 1

VIDEO LISTENING GUIDE

1. Jesus restored the keys of <u>authority</u> to humanity and commissioned us to go.
2. Since God's original design and plan, <u>sin</u> had entered the world.
3. Since Jesus has all authority, the devil has <u>no</u> authority.
4. God called and positioned mankind to be the <u>delegated</u> authority over the planet.
5. God is raising up a company of people to bring divine <u>order</u> back to the planet.
6. Jesus performed His miracles as a <u>man</u>, not as God.

Week 2

YOUR SIGNIFICANCE IN HIS PRESENCE

* ***Prayer Focus:*** Ask the Lord to establish each participant in the Truth that they are worthy to be used by God to do the extraordinary *because* they have received the Holy Spirit.

Fellowship and Welcome (10-15 Minutes)

- Welcome everyone as they walk in. Be sure to identify any new members who were not at the previous session, and be sure that they receive the appropriate materials—workbook and book.
- In the small group, serve refreshments and facilitate fellowship between group members. In a class setting, talk with the attendees—ask how their week has been and maintain a focus on what God has done and is doing. It is easy for people to go off into what they perceive has not happened, or focus on the negative. Rather than pretend that the negative is not there, it is essential to cultivate an atmosphere of faith and expectation before the session even begins. If there are prayer needs, address those during the designated prayer time. Again, it is essential to create an atmosphere of faith so that when it comes to the prayer/activation time, there is boldness and expectancy in the prayers.
- Encourage everyone to congregate in the meeting place. If it is a classroom setting, make an announcement that it is time to sit down and begin the session. If it is a small group, ensure everyone makes their way to the designated meeting space.

Opening Prayer

Worship (15-20 Minutes)

(Note: Specifically, for this session, it is recommended that you engage the worship component at the end of the meeting instead of at the beginning. However, if you are accustomed to opening the meeting in worship, perhaps shorten the time, allowing for some time at the end of the meeting for some additional worship.)

When it comes to the worship element, it can be executed in both small group and church class settings. While a worship time is not mandatory, it is highly encouraged, as the fundamental goal of this curriculum is to increase each participant's hunger for the Presence of God. Worship is a wonderful way of opening each session and setting everyone's perspective on what the class is about—not accumulating more information, but pursuing greater encounters in God's Presence.

In fact, starting Week 2 with a time of worship ideally sets the stage for the topic of discussion—the believer's significance is found in his or her identity as a priest unto God. To be a worshipper is to step into a very significant role, as one who ministers directly to the Lord.

Prayer/Ministry Time (5-15 Minutes)

Video/Teaching (20 Minutes)

Discussion Questions (25-30 Minutes)

- What does it mean to "empower the liar" by agreeing with a lie?
  - ANSWER: As we have discovered, Jesus possesses all authority. If Jesus has all authority, the enemy has none—except what mankind gives to him through believing his lies.
  - One of the enemy's key lies to the Body of Christ is the lie of insignificance. He is very proactive, trying to get believers to buy into the lie that they are not significant, when, in fact, the blood of Jesus has made them *priests* unto God. Significance is in a believer's very identity.
- *Read Exodus 19:6 and Isaiah 61:6.* What is God's will for His people according to these passages? (Specifically, what ministry has He called all believers to?)
  - ANSWER: He desires a people of priests. In other words, His will is for a people who minister directly to Him, who have access to His Presence, and are able to worship Him face to face.
- *Read First Peter 2:9.* How have all believers become priests unto God?
  - ANSWER: In the Old Testament, God spoke prophetically about the identity that He desired His people to step into. Because of the redemptive work of Christ, every single

believer is now able to occupy the role of "priest," ministering directly to the Lord, in His Presence.

- What are the key ministries of priests? How do we function in those roles today?
    - ANSWER: The key ministries of priests, according to the video session, are to minister to a) God, and b) people. When it comes to breaking down ministry to people, it can be divided into two categories: a) ministry to believers (the Church), and b) ministry to the world (unbelievers).
- What is the difference between thanksgiving, praise, and worship?
    - ANSWER: Thanksgiving is man's response to God's acts (what God has done). Praise is focused on God's nature (who He is). Worship is a lifestyle.
    - While we read about sacrifices of praise and thanksgiving, there is no mention of a "sacrifice of worship," because *we are the sacrifice* (see Rom. 12:1).

Activate: Step Into Your Identity (10 Minutes)

- Worship and minister unto the Lord. Take some time at the end of the meeting for some additional praise and worship. Perhaps do one normal praise/worship chorus, and follow it up with some spontaneous/prophetic worship, giving people the opportunity to connect with God personally and individually—thus fulfilling their priestly identity, ministering directly unto the Lord.
- Again, this is an ideal time to listen to the Holy Spirit and ask specifically for what He wants to say or do. People may start giving/receiving prophetic words. There may be a gift of healing that is released. The key in this session is not pursuing gifts or manifestations; they come second. As the group focuses on the Presence on the Presence and ministering directly to the Lord, the Holy Spirit comes and empowers the participants for ministry to each other.

TAKE AWAY

Before we are positioned to release His Presence to the world and impact our spheres of influence, it is vital that we recognize our significance as believers. Because of Jesus' work, we are priests unto God. We minister directly to Him, in His Presence. It is out of that place that we are empowered to minister in the "outer courts" to people, both in the Church and in the world.

Plans for the Next Week (2 Minutes)

Encourage group members to stay up to date with their daily exercises in the *Hosting the Presence Workbook.*

Close in Prayer

Week 2

VIDEO LISTENING GUIDE

1. In redemption, we are restored to an identity greater than before the Fall.
2. The enemy enters our lives through agreement.
3. We empower the liar through our agreement with his lies.
4. We have been called by God to be priests unto the Lord.
5. Two ministries of priests:
    a. To God.
    b. To people.
6. Two ministries to people:
    a. To believers.
    b. To the world.
7. We always become like whatever we worship.
8. Thanksgiving is our response to God's acts.
9. Praise is focused on God's nature.
10. In worship, we are the sacrifice.

Week 3

Empowered by His Presence

Prayer Focus: Ask the Lord to open each participant's eyes to the reality that they are empowered by God's Presence to overcome fear and accomplish the impossible!

Fellowship and Welcome (10-15 Minutes)

- Welcome everyone as they walk in. Be sure to identify any new members who were not at the previous session, and be sure that they receive the appropriate materials—workbook and book.
- Encourage everyone to congregate in the meeting place. If it is a classroom setting, make an announcement that it is time to sit down and begin the session. If it is a small group, ensure everyone makes their way to the designated meeting space.

Opening Prayer

Worship (15-20 Minutes)

Prayer/Ministry Time (5-15 Minutes)

Video/Teaching (20 Minutes)

Discussion Questions (25-30 Minutes)

- *Read Judges 6:10.* One of the first things God instructs Gideon to do is "not fear." How can fear restrict people from accomplishing God's purposes?
    - ANSWER: The key is not to focus *too long* on the problem—fear—as the key to this session is addressing the solution: the reality that the God of the impossible empowers us to accomplish His purposes.

- This is more of a subjective question and is designed to open conversation about the topic of facing fear through embracing identity.

- *Read Judges 6:11-12.* God calls Gideon a "mighty man of valor" while he is hiding in fear. Jesus called Peter a rock when his name meant "broken reed." What does it mean that God has a name for you that is the opposite of your greatest weakness?

    - ANSWER: God knows what is inside of us, especially now that the Spirit of God is inside of us. He knows exactly what the Presence-empowered believer is able to accomplish: the impossible. God does not call us by what we are experiencing or dealing with or wading through; He calls us according to how He sees us.

- *Read Judges 6:34.* In the Amplified Bible, it says that the Spirit of the Lord "clothed Gideon with Himself."

- Share about a time where you felt like the Holy Spirit "clothed" Himself with you, and used you to accomplish something impossible.

    - This will be the final question (and will flow right into the activation time), so be sure to spend a good amount of time here, encouraging everyone to share testimonies of how God used them to accomplish the impossible, especially in spite of their weaknesses! The key is to let testimonies build an atmosphere of faith, expectation, and encouragement.

    - ANSWER: With more subjective questions like this one, it is important to ensure that no single group members "hog the spotlight." There are people who like to talk more than others—which is fine. The key is making sure everyone feels heard and that everyone has an appropriate amount of time to share what is on his or her heart, as this is a time of testimony sharing.

- Transition right into activation time!

Activate: Call Forth Empowered Identity! (10 Minutes)

- Pray specifically for divine setups where the Spirit of God has the opportunity to use each member mightily—like Gideon—to accomplish something supernatural and impossible.

- Open the meeting for people to prophesy identity over one another. Have participants call out the things within each other that God has placed there.
(Note: If certain group members are not familiar with the prophetic or calling out words of knowledge, invite group members to share a word of "encouragement" with their fellow participants, as directed by the Holy Spirit. Sometimes, the only thing that holds people

back from ministering supernaturally is the "language barrier." The term "prophesy" may make some people feel uneasy, but "Spirit-led encouragement" does not. Then, after they deliver a word, you can encourage them that what they just did was flow in the prophetic according to First Corinthians 14:3.)

TAKE AWAY

Gideon is an Old Testament prototype of what all believers have access to today—the ability to be empowered by the Presence of God to accomplish the impossible. Remember, God does not look at our weaknesses; He looks at our Presence-empowered potential and calls it out!

Plans for the Next Week (2 Minutes)

Encourage group members to stay up to date with their daily exercises in the *Hosting the Presence Workbook.*

Close in Prayer

Week 3

VIDEO LISTENING GUIDE

1. What you fear infects what you worship.
2. God has a name for you that is the opposite of your greatest weakness.
3. God wants to use your uniqueness to illustrate His message.

Week 4

A Sneak Preview of God's House

Prayer Focus: Ask the Holy Spirit to give each participant revelation and understanding, as the following session is going to challenge their paradigms and enhance how they observe the "house of God."

Fellowship and Welcome (10-15 Minutes)

- Welcome everyone as they walk in. Be sure to identify any new members who were not at the previous session, and be sure that they receive the appropriate materials—workbook and book.
- Encourage everyone to congregate in the meeting place. If it is a classroom setting, make an announcement that it is time to sit down and begin the session. If it is a small group, ensure everyone makes their way to the designated meeting space.

Opening Prayer

Worship (15-20 Minutes)

Prayer/Ministry Time (5-15 Minutes)

Video/Teaching (25 Minutes)

Discussion Questions (25-30 Minutes)

- *Read Genesis 28:12-13,17.* In Jacob's dream of the ladder into heaven, what were the three things he specifically saw that defined the house of God?

  ANSWER: An open heaven, angelic activity (ascending and descending), and hearing the voice of God.

- This is worthy of our attention because this is the first mention of the "house of God" in Scripture.

▪ *Read Genesis 28:17 again.* Jacob identified this place as the "house of God" and the "gate of heaven." How can the house of God be a gate?

ANSWER: It comes down to understanding what the house of God is. In the Old Testament, it was initially revealed as a gateway between two realms. There was no building; there was only Jacob and God.

▪ Bill Johnson defines the house of God as "built on the edge of two worlds." What does this mean to you?

ANSWER: The house of God is a gateway, or a transition point, bringing the resources, power, and government of one world (heaven) into another (earth).

▪ *Read John 1:48-51.* How does Jesus bring initial fulfillment to Jacob's dream in Genesis 28?

ANSWER: Jesus' language demonstrates prophetic (but partial) fulfillment of what Jacob saw in his dream. Jesus is the ladder connecting heaven to earth. Jesus, through His baptism in the Holy Spirit, experiences a consistent flow of supernatural resources/angelic activity originating in one world (heaven) and being released on earth (producing signs, wonders, miracles, etc.).

- The key is understanding that Jesus was the *initial* fulfillment—not the final—to Jacob's prophetic dream.

▪ How do you think Jacob's dream is still being fulfilled in our generation (even after Christ left the earth)?

ANSWER: The goal is to get the participants to see that the fulfillment of Jacob's dream of "the house of God" is in them—the Body of Christ, the Church. Not a building or organization, per se, but the Body of Presence-filled believers spanning the globe.

▪ *Review the Acts 2 Pentecost experience.* What were the similarities between the birth of the Church on Pentecost and Jacob's dream in Genesis 28?

ANSWER: A sound from an open heaven (see Acts 2:2), and fire—representing supernatural/angelic activity (see Acts 2:3).

Activate: Open Up the Gates! (10 Minutes)

- Pray that believers across the earth would step into the "house of God" identity revealed in Scripture: walking under an open heaven, hearing the voice of God, and experiencing the supernatural. You might want to have group members and class participants lay hands on each other to release impartation, or you may prefer to have a leader lay hands on each of the participants.

- Since every person in the group is a believer (most likely), invite the Holy Spirit to come and make each participant aware of 1) the open heaven over his or her life, 2) their ability to hear God's voice, and 3) their inheritance to move in the supernatural.
(Note: In any instance of this kind, be prepared to appropriately steward the atmosphere. This means listening to the Holy Spirit, yielding to His move, and, in part, pastoring the people who are present. Simply ask the Holy Spirit what He is doing and He will faithfully reveal to you which way He is going, even if it is in a moment-to-moment manner.)

TAKE AWAY

Jacob received a prophetic blueprint for the normal Christian life in Genesis 28. Jesus was the initial fulfillment and model. But ultimately, even He pointed to the Presence-empowered community of believers—the Church—as the house of God. Such is characterized by an open heaven, the voice of God, and a continuous flow of the supernatural/angelic activity from one world to the other.

Plans for the Next Week (2 Minutes)

Encourage group members to stay up to date with their daily exercises in the *Hosting the Presence Workbook.*

Close in Prayer

Week 4

VIDEO LISTENING GUIDE

1. The house of God has:
   a. An open heaven.
   b. Angelic activity.
   c. The voice of God.
2. A gate is a transition place from one realm to another.
3. God has built His house on the edge of two worlds.
4. Jesus becomes the initial fulfillment of the house of God prophesied in the Old Testament.
5. Earth invaded heaven before heaven invaded earth.

Week 5

THE ANSWER TO ANCIENT CRIES

Prayer Focus: Ask the Lord to establish each participant in the reality that they walk under open heavens where the supernatural is readily accessible.

Fellowship and Welcome (10-15 Minutes)

- Welcome everyone as they walk in. Be sure to identify any new members who were not at the previous session, and be sure that they receive the appropriate materials—workbook and book.
- Encourage everyone to congregate in the meeting place. If it is a classroom setting, make an announcement that it is time to sit down and begin the session. If it is a small group, ensure everyone makes their way to the designated meeting space.

Opening Prayer

Worship (15-20 Minutes)

Prayer/Ministry Time (5-15 Minutes)

Video/Teaching (20 Minutes)

Discussion Questions (25-30 Minutes)

- *Read Isaiah 64:1 and Mark 1:10.* How is Isaiah 64:1 fulfilled in Jesus' baptism?
    - ANSWER: Isaiah 64:1 represents the Old Testament cry for God to "rend the heavens" and come down. Jesus was the New Testament answer to this cry; for on the day of His baptism, the heavens were violently torn open as the Spirit of God

descended upon Him and remained. This represents God's will for man—that the Spirit of God would rest and remain upon every believer.

- How was the release of God's Spirit into the earth aimed at the powers of darkness?

    - ANSWER: Because of Jesus, the Holy Spirit has been released into the earth and He is the personification of light. Every power of darkness has become set up for destruction, because now every believer lives under an open heaven, is filled with the Holy Spirit, and is empowered to release that Presence into the earth, bringing about supernatural transformation.

- What does the following mean to you: "Most closed heavens are between the ears for believers"?

    - ANSWER: "Between the ears" refers to the mind—namely the unrenewed mind. Because of Jesus, heaven is opened over every single believer. Period. The problem is that many believers do not believe that heaven is opened and that the supernatural is easily accessible. This is why many people pray and ask for what they have already received through inheritance.

- What is the difference between the Holy Spirit living *within* and resting *upon* you?

    - ANSWER: The Holy Spirit lives inside of every born-again believer; however, the reality of the Holy Spirit resting *upon* believers is much different. It has everything to do with how much a believer allows the Holy Spirit to flow *through* them.

- Why do we invite the Holy Spirit to come when He is already living inside of us and God is omnipresent (present everywhere)? *Read Isaiah 6:1.*

    - ANSWER: God fills...and continues to fill. He comes, but there is still more of Him yet to come. Due to God's sheer volume, size, and scope, it is ignorant for us to assume that our current experience of God is everything there is to be accessed and enjoyed.

- Describe a time when you experienced the Holy Spirit resting *upon* you, where you knew that God was speaking, ministering, healing, or working *through* you.

    - ANSWER: Subjective.

- Can you share about a time where you experienced the Holy Spirit *filling* a place? How did it feel and what happened?

- ANSWER: Subjective. However, feel free to spend some time on this question, perhaps getting two to three group members to share their testimonies. Again, the goal is to stir faith in the participants as they hear their peers share about real life encounters and experiences they have had with God. Transition immediately from this question to the activation time, as the goal is for everyone to experience—in some measure—what has been shared about in the testimony time.

Activate: The Heavens Are Opened! (10 Minutes)

- Pray for increased awareness of the reality that every believer walks and lives under—heaven has been opened for 2,000 years and is accessible to every person who has been born again!
- Invite each group member to lay hands on the person to their left or right (figure out the most orderly way to do this in the context of your group). Ask them to pray for increase. Remember, they do not need more of the Holy Spirit; they have received Him in full. The key is experiencing and releasing what they have already received in an increased measure.
- (Note: Again, how this activation time is executed depends on your group size and structure. However, for this study to be most effective, it is recommended that you consistently engage the activation exercises with your groups/class, as it allows them to put hands and feet to what they just learned. One of the main goals of these activation exercises is to engage *every* participant and show them that they too are able to pray, prophesy, impart, and exhort—and do so boldly! Too many are stuck in a rut where they believe the privilege of supernatural ministry belongs only to those in the pulpit.

TAKE AWAY

Isaiah 64:1 represents the generational cry of God's people to see Him come down and move in power among them. Because of Jesus, this cry has been fulfilled. He modeled the anointed, Presence-empowered Christian life, and then, because of His redemptive work, made a way for every believer to walk under an open heaven—experiencing and releasing the supernatural power of God *today*!

Plans for the Next Week (2 Minutes)

Encourage group members to stay up to date with their daily exercises in the *Hosting the Presence Workbook.*

Close in Prayer

Week 5

VIDEO LISTENING GUIDE

1. The Holy Spirit lives inside of every believer, but He does not rest upon every believer.
2. A key to hosting the Presence of God: take every step with the dove in mind.
3. When we are conscious of an open heaven, we live differently.
4. Jesus did not live in reaction to darkness; He lived responding to the Father.
5. There is a difference between what we have in our possession and what we have in our account.
6. Every outpouring of the Holy Spirit contains the face of God.

Week 6

THE PROTOTYPE FOR NORMAL CHRISTIANITY

Prayer Focus: Ask the Lord to give everyone a clear picture of what the normal Christian life looks like—a people ordained and assigned to host and carry God's Presence with their lives.

Fellowship and Welcome (10-15 Minutes)

- Welcome everyone as they walk in. Be sure to identify any new members who were not at the previous session, and be sure that they receive the appropriate materials—workbook and book.
- Encourage everyone to congregate in the meeting place. If it is a classroom setting, make an announcement that it is time to sit down and begin the session. If it is a small group, ensure everyone makes their way to the designated meeting space.

Opening Prayer

Worship (5-10 Minutes)

For this particular session, we recommend starting with a shorter time of praise and worship, and then incorporating another worship set into your activation time at the end.

Prayer/Ministry Time (5-15 Minutes)

Video/Teaching (20 Minutes)

Discussion Questions (25-30 Minutes)

- *Read Second Samuel 6:6-8.* Uzzah was struck dead because he improperly handled the Presence of God. What does Bill Johnson mean when he says, "The Presence of the Lord was never meant to rest on something that man creates"?

  - ANSWER: The problem comes when people start believing their ministry, building, or organization is *the* vehicle that carries God's Presence. Man starts believing the work of his hands was worthy of God's abiding Presence. This is not so, as God's original intention was never to dwell in a house made of brick and stone. He is not contained by a structure. Rather, He desires a unique dwelling place (which we will learn about).

- *Read Acts 15:16-17 and Amos 9:11-12.* What is significant about the Tabernacle of David that separates it from how worship was traditionally performed under the Old Covenant?

  - ANSWER: The sacrifice was different and the protocol for experiencing God's Presence was different. Rather than the blood of animals and the work of atonement being executed by the priests, the focus was prophetic. In the context of the Tabernacle of David, there were the priests, there was constant worship, and there was the Presence of God. This would point to the era of Pentecost (and thereafter), as defined in Acts 15:16-17.

- How is the Tabernacle of David a prototype or preview of the New Testament Church?

  - ANSWER: In the New Testament Church, the work of atonement has been performed by Jesus. His once-and-for-all sacrifice made a way for people to be saved, to be filled with His Spirit, and to occupy the role of priests, ministering unto the Lord—in His Presence—and ministering to the people by *releasing* His Presence. In the Tabernacle of David, there were priests, there was praise, and there was the Presence of God. The same is true for us today!

- *Read Second Samuel 6:15-16.* What are some expressions of praise and worship that may appear foolish to outsiders (either unbelievers or people trapped in a religious perspective)?

  - ANSWER: Subjective. Have each participant provide his or her perspective.

- How do expressions of praise and worship (for example, dancing) open the door for God's Presence to move?

  - ANSWER: For example, "David danced before the Lord's Presence" (see 2 Sam. 6:14). He danced "before" the Lord, not after. In other words, authentic praise and worship always come before God shows up. It's easy to praise and worship *when*

He comes; however, His Presence actually responds to the praises that go before His arrival.

- Share about a time in praise and worship where you experienced God's Presence entering into that environment *after* people started praising. What happened and how did His Presence change things?

    - ANSWER: Subjective. After everyone has responded and you sense faith and expectation filling the room, transition immediately into the activation time. (Start with one or two songs of worship.)

Activate: Praising Before the Presence (10 Minutes)

- As a group, sing one or two worship songs, specifically themed on inviting the Presence of the Lord into that environment. You can do one formal chorus, and then transition into a more spontaneous/soaking type of song if you feel it is appropriate. The key is to show each participant how to praise God before the Presence shows up, taking their place as the modern Tabernacle of David.
- Ensure that they understand their praise carries national and global implications. Powers, principalities, and darkness are actually subdued by the Church's praise and worship. The key is taking it beyond just "singing a song," or even singing with excitement and passion, to recognizing that worship is the conduit for the Presence of God to inhabit people, buildings, atmospheres, regions, and even nations.
- After praise and worship, evaluate the atmosphere. What do you feel directed by the Holy Spirit to do (or not do)? It is important to flow with the anointing and follow the leading of the Holy Spirit.
- (Note: Just because the Presence of the Lord shows up does not necessarily mean you always have to *do* something—like prophesy, pray, lay hands, dance, shout, etc. Sometimes, He simply wants us to rest in His Presence, enjoy His glory, and remain still. Let's not be like Peter at the Mount of Transfiguration, where he had a powerful encounter with God's glory, and because he did not know what to say, he proposed a tabernacle building project for Jesus, Elijah, and Moses.)

TAKE AWAY

The Tabernacle of David is an Old Testament prototype for what the New Testament Church should look and function like. In this Tabernacle, there were priests, praise, and Presence. The same should characterize the modern Body of Christ. Every believer is a priest with the ability to praise that has the potential to access and release God's Presence—individually, corporately, congregationally, regionally, and even globally!

Plans for the Next Week (2 Minutes)

Encourage group members to stay up to date with their daily exercises in the *Hosting the Presence Workbook.*

Close in Prayer

Week 6

VIDEO LISTENING GUIDE

1. The Presence of the Lord was never meant to rest on something man creates.
2. The Presence of God rests on people, not ministries.
3. The Tabernacle of David is the prototype for the New Testament Church.
4. David danced before the Presence, not after.
5. Worship appears foolish to those not participating in it.

Week 7

KEYS TO PRACTICALLY RELEASING GOD'S PRESENCE

Prayer Focus: Ask the Lord to empower and embolden every participant to step out and release God's Presence through the keys they are going to learn in this session.

Fellowship and Welcome (10-15 Minutes)

- Welcome everyone as they walk in. Be sure to identify any new members who were not at the previous session, and be sure that they receive the appropriate materials—workbook and book.
- Encourage everyone to congregate in the meeting place. If it is a classroom setting, make an announcement that it is time to sit down and begin the session. If it is a small group, ensure everyone makes their way to the designated meeting space.

Opening Prayer

Worship (15-20 Minutes)

Prayer/Ministry Time (5-15 Minutes)

Video/Teaching (20 Minutes)

Discussion Questions (25-30 Minutes)

- *Read Mark 6:56.* How did the woman's testimony (who was healed of the issue of blood) appear to impact people throughout the area?

- ANSWER: According to Mark 6:56, Jesus' entry into villages, cities, and the country was greeted by people who sought to "just touch the hem of His garment." They were not necessarily applying some type of formula. Rather, they were stirred by the woman's testimony and they knew there was something special about this Man—so much so, that even the clothes He wore released Presence and power.

- We should not get distracted by the hem of Jesus' garment. Rather, it was the Presence upon Him that caused His very clothes to release power. This is what the woman was placing her faith in. She heard testimony of this Man, Jesus, and knew there was something special about Him—His very Presence—that released life and healing. This stirred her faith, so much so, that she believed that His Presence was so powerful, even touching the hem of his garment would release healing. She was right!

- *Read Acts 19:11-12.* Cloths and handkerchiefs that were on Paul's body possessed healing power. How did this work, and what does it mean for us today?

  - ANSWER: The garments from Paul's body that were used to release healing and deliverance were not necessarily special "prayer cloths." Rather, they were the clothes and sweatbands he wore during his normal, everyday life. While he was working and building tents, these were the articles of clothing that he wore. This demonstrates the degree to which someone can host God's Presence in one's everyday sphere of influence.

  - Just like the hem of Jesus' garment should not distract us, we should not focus on anointed clothes either. Rather, we should pursue a lifestyle where we are so smeared and overshadowed by God's Presence that everything about us releases supernatural power and changes the atmosphere around us.

- What does the following statement mean to you: "Breakthrough does not always come through instruction; often, it comes through adventure" (Bill Johnson)?

  - ANSWER: The anointed clothes, from the hem of Jesus' garment to Paul's garments, were not tools used to heal the sick based on principles. Like Bill Johnson said, Paul did not have some type of teaching series or seminar where he included anointed clothes as a tool to release breakthrough. This discovery, that Presence could actually be transferred through touch and anointed cloth, was identified through adventure. Through testing. Through putting two and two together.

  - All of the methods you will learn about for releasing God's Presence come through both instruction and discovery/adventure.

- *Read John 6:63 and Romans 14:17.* When we say what the Father is saying and make decrees, we release the Presence and advance the Kingdom. Remember, the Kingdom of God is released *in* the Presence of the Holy Spirit.
- Share a time where your words/prayers/decrees released the Presence of God into a situation or upon a person. What happened?
    - ANSWER: Subjective.
- This week in your workbook, you will be going through all of the keys that release God's Presence—*intentional* and *unintentional*. Today, we focused on the unintentional method of releasing God's Presence through clothing.
- Based on the model of Jesus and the early Church, share what you think some of the other methods are.
    - ANSWER: Word/decree, act of faith, prophetic act, touch, shadow, compassion, clothing, and worship.

Activate: Releasing the Presence (10 Minutes)

- Encourage group members to share prayer requests.
- Be adventurous and practice different methods of releasing God's Presence to address the mentioned prayer requests. (For example: have some members lay hands on those who are sick; have some pray prayers of decree concerning the will of God for the specified prayer request; and for those who know people who need breakthrough—but are not currently attending the group—release God's Presence over cloths that can be used as a point of contact.)

TAKE AWAY

The key is not becoming overly focused on the specific method of releasing God's Presence—whether it would be through decree, prophetic acts, faith, anointed cloths, etc. The focus must always be the Presence of God that empowers the method, as methods are subject to change, even on a situational basis. In fact, God will most likely introduce you to new, potentially unusual methods of releasing His Presence. If the focus is always Him, however, then there is always room to be adventurous in the methods—just as long as they do not distract from His Presence, His work, and His Word.

Plans for the Next Week (2 Minutes)

Encourage group members to stay up to date with their daily exercises in the *Hosting the Presence Workbook.*

Close in Prayer

Week 7

VIDEO LISTENING GUIDE

1. This breakthrough did not come through instruction; it came through adventure.
2. Your shadow will always release what overshadows you.
3. The dove is always looking for a place to rest.
4. The Holy Spirit lives inside of us for our sake; but He is upon us for everyone else.
5. The Kingdom of God is in the Holy Spirit.
6. Ways to release God's Presence:
    a. Word.
    b. Touch.
    c. The prophetic act.
    d. Act of faith.

Week 8

YOUR BAPTISM OF FIRE

Prayer Focus: Ask the Lord to come and manifest His Presence, stirring more hunger in every participant for deeper encounters with Him.

Fellowship and Welcome (10-15 Minutes)

- Welcome everyone as they walk in. Be sure to identify any new members who were not at the previous session, and be sure that they receive the appropriate materials—workbook and book.
- Encourage everyone to congregate in the meeting place. If it is a classroom setting, make an announcement that it is time to sit down and begin the session. If it is a small group, ensure everyone makes their way to the designated meeting space.

Opening Prayer

Linger a little bit longer in the opening prayer, as you feel led. The Holy Spirit might begin stirring hunger even prior to watching the video.

Worship (15-20 Minutes)

No Prayer/Ministry Time

This will be reserved for the end.

Video/Teaching (20 Minutes)

This lesson is very unique, as it features Bill Johnson sharing his personal testimony of experiencing God's Presence in a life-changing, personal encounter.

This particular segment will focus more on ministry, prayer, and activation than discussion questions, which is why there are no questions listed below. There are also no interactive questions for the participants to respond to while watching this session.

No Discussion Questions

Activate: Releasing the Presence (20-30 Minutes)

- TRANSITION: Immediately after watching the DVD session, encourage everyone to enter into a posture and attitude of hunger/expectancy.
- WORSHIP: If possible, you can lightly play some worship music in the background. You can use either a CD, or have someone who is musically inclined and sensitive to the flow of the Holy Spirit play a keyboard or guitar in the background. The key is the music flowing with the Holy Spirit and enhancing what He is doing, not distracting from it.
- DIRECTION: Group members are going to pray in small groups. We want them to:

    1) Pray for an increased hunger for each other to experience and release God's Presence.

    2) Pray that the encounters they experience in private with God's Presence embolden them to take greater risks in public, and release His Presence over people who need an encounter with Him.

    3) As the Spirit directs, encourage group members to prophesy and encourage one another through words of knowledge, etc.

(Note: Again, the litmus test for prophetic words is encouragement and exhortation.)

- PRAYER/ENCOUNTER: Have group members gather together in groups of three and pray for one another. If there needs to be one group of two people, that's fine (or a single group of four is also fine). Have them follow the instructions listed above.
- During this time, you—the group leader/class instructor—will serve as a facilitator, navigating the direction the Holy Spirit wants to take the group in as a whole.
- Remember to monitor the individual groups, and ensure that the ministry taking place is exhorting, encouraging, and hunger-stirring.
- Be sure to prepare for certain manifestations of God's Presence. People may fall, so be sure there are blankets nearby. People may start laughing, shaking or weeping, and in this context that is perfectly acceptable. If there are group members who may not be familiar with this type of manifestation, be sure to provide some brief instruction.

TAKE AWAY

Bill Johnson's testimony is prophetic. When someone shares of his or her encounter with God, it releases an invitation for every person within hearing distance to hunger for what that person experienced. God is intensely personal, so we should not expect the identical encounters as others experience, just as Bill encourages. Each encounter is dramatic; whether we experience something physically electrifying or receive a simple Word from Scripture that goes on to define the way we do life and ministry.

Plans for the Next Week (2 Minutes)

Let participants know that either this is the final week of the study or you will be having some type of social activity on the following week—or at a specified future date.

Close in Prayer

Pray that the increased measure of hunger for God's Presence would be experienced and released in the group members' individual, everyday lives.

Hunger for God's Presence cannot end when the 40-day journey concludes and the group/class finishes up. This is only the beginning of a new level of encounter and release of God's Presence in each person's unique sphere of influence.

LOOKING FOR MORE FROM BILL JOHNSON AND BETHEL CHURCH?

Purchase additional resources—CDs, DVDs, digital downloads, music—from Bill Johnson and the Bethel team at the Bethel store.

Visit www.bjm.org for more information on Bill Johnson, to view his speaking itinerary, or to look into additional teaching resources.

To order Bethel Church resources, visit http://store.ibethel.org

Subscribe to iBethel.TV to access the latest sermons, worship sets, and conferences from Bethel Church.

To subscribe, visit www.ibethel.tv

Become part of a Supernatural Culture that is transforming the world and apply to the Bethel School of Supernatural Ministry.

For more information, visit www.ibethel.org/school-of-ministry

Made in the USA
Coppell, TX
13 February 2023